PHONICS :LEARN ENGLISH READING IN JUST 90 DAYS

By Raut Seema

To Parents ,Teachers

Dear Readers,

Thank you for choosing this phonics Book as part of your learning journey!

As an author and educator, I am excited to share this 90-day course designed to help your 5- 14 year-old child master 100% English reading. Over the course of 90 days, your child will progress from basic reading skills to advanced fluency.

Currently, I am teaching this course through online classes to students from various schools. However, to reach a broader audience and make learning accessible for all, I decided to create this book. It is designed for teachers offering private lessons, so they can use this resource to teach students effectively.

This book covers the complete syllabus, from foundational reading skills to advanced reading abilities. Additionally, it includes essential reading rules that will empower children to become independent readers.

For best results, it is crucial to follow the books in the order provided, starting with the first edition and progressing through to the last edition. Equally important is daily practice — just 10 minutes a day can make a significant difference.By the end of this course, your child will have the confidence to read independently from any book. This approach guarantees that your child will be well on their way to becoming a fluent reader in English.

Sincerely,

[Raut.S.S]

Author & Educator

In this course, you should teach children English Reading by following these steps:

Step 1: Ensure children know the A to Z letters sound.

Step 2: Teach children to read CVC (Consonant-Vowel-Consonant) words.

Step 3: Begin teaching the " R " " S" " L" blends and have children read

all the words related to this blend provided in the book. If your child struggles with a word, help them sound it out.

Step 4: If a word cannot be sounded out (such as "the" ,"once"), say it

out loud and have your child repeat it.

Step 5: Have children read the sentences provided in the book. If

your child struggles with a word, help them sound it out.

Step 6: Encourage children to practice writing the all " R " " S" " L" blend.

Step 7: Have children independently identify and underline all " R " " S" " L" blends in the text.

Note- In this book, our focus is solely on teaching the " R " " S" " L" blends. The next part of the syllabus will be introduced in the upcoming Book No2. Our primary goal here is for children to understand and master only the " R " " S" " L" blends.

Content

Brief overview of the sounds associated with each letter:

A a: /a/ as in "apple"

B b: /b/ as in "ball"

C c: /c/ as in "cat"

D d: /d/ as in "dog"

E e: /e/ as in "egg"

F f: /f/ as in "fish"

G g: /g/ as in "go"

H h: /h/ as in "hat"

I i: /ɪ/ as in "in"

J j: /j/ as in "jump"

K k: /k/ as in "kite"

L l: /l/ as in "lamp"

M m: /m/ as in "mouse"

N n: /n/ as in "net"

O o: /o/ as in "orange"

P p: /p/ as in "pig"

Q q: /q/ as in "queen"

R r: /r/ as in "rabbit"

S s: /s/ as in "sun"

T t: /t/ as in "top"

U u: /u/ as in "umbrella"

V v: /v/ as in "van"

W w: /w/ as in "water"

X x: /ks/ as in "box"

Y y: /y/ as in "yellow"

Z z: /z/ as in "zebra"

Say Sounds

Aa	Bb	Cc	Dd	Ee
Ff	Gg	Hh	Ii	Jj
Kk	Ll	Mm	Nn	Oo
Pp	Qq	Rr	Ss	Tt
Uu	Vv	Ww	Xx	Yy
Zz				

Revision

A CVC Words (Word Families):

-at: Cat, Bat, Rat, Hat, Mat, Fat, Sat, Pat

-an: Man, Can, Ran, Fan, Pan, Van, Tan, Ban

-ap: Cap, Map, Nap, Tap, Lap, Sap, Gap, Zap

-ag: Bag, Rag, Tag, Wag, Lag, Nag

-am: Ram, Jam, Ham, Yam, Cam, Bam, Sam

E CVC Words (Word Families):

-et: Bet, Jet, Set, Let, Get, Net, Pet, Met

-en: Hen, Men, Ten, Pen, Den, Ken

-ed: Red, Bed, Fed, Led, Ted, Ned

-eg: Leg, Peg, Beg, Meg

-em: Gem, Hem

I CVC Words (Word Families):

-it: Bit, Fit, Hit, Kit, Lit, Pit, Sit, Zit

-in: Pin, Win, Bin, Fin, Sin, Tin

-ig: Big, Dig, Fig, Wig, Pig, Jig

-ip: Lip, Zip, Tip, Sip, Hip, Dip

-im: Him, Rim, Dim, Sim

O CVC Words (Word Families):

-ot: Hot, Not, Pot, Rot, Lot, Cot, Dot, Got

-op: Hop, Mop, Top, Pop, Cop, Sop, Bop

-og: Dog, Fog, Log, Jog, Hog, Bog

-ob: Cob, Rob, Job, Sob

-ox: Box, Fox, Lox

U CVC Words (Word Families):

-ut: Cut, Hut, Nut, But, Gut

-un: Fun, Sun, Run, Bun, Gun

-ug: Bug, Dug, Hug, Jug, Rug, Tug

-ub: Cub, Tub, Sub, Hub, Rub

-um: Gum, Hum, Sum, Mum

Phonics " R "Blends Guide

What is a Blend? A blend is when two or more consonants come together to create a new sound. For example, in the word "br" (as in "brown"), the letters "b" and "r" combine to make one sound.

How to Pronounce Blends:

1. Start Slowly:

Begin by saying each consonant sound slowly. For example, for br, say "b-b-r" and then blend them together until it sounds like "br."

2. Practice with Your Mouth:

Pay attention to how your mouth moves when saying each blend. For the fr sound, your upper teeth should gently touch your bottom lip to make the "f" sound before quickly adding the "r."

Tips for Mastering "R" Blends:

1. Use Visuals:

Associate each blend with a picture. For example, "br" can be linked to a picture of a brown bear.

2. Repeat Words:Practice saying words with the same blend.

Make it a fun game to say words with the br blend (e.g., "bread," "bricks," and "broom") and see how fast you can say them!

Common "R" Blends:

1. Br- Blend:

The sound made when the letters b and r come together.

Example words: bread, broom, bricks.

2. Cr- Blend:

The sound made when the letters c and r come together.

Example words: crab, cream, crayon.

3. Fr- Blend:

The sound made when the letters f and r come together.

Example words: frog, fruit, french.

4. Dr- Blend:

The sound made when the letters d and r come together.

Example words: drum, dress, drive.

5. Gr- Blend:

The sound made when the letters g and r come together.

Example words: grass, great, group.

6.Pr- Blend:

The sound made when the letters p and r come together.

Example words: princess, pram, prawn.

7.. Wr- Blend:

The sound made when the letters w and r come together.

Example words: wrap, write, wreck.

How to Pronounce Hard and Soft C & G:

1. Hard C:

When C is followed by a, o, or u, say the hard /k/ sound. For example, for cat, say "k" followed by the rest of the word.

2. Soft C:

sound. For example, for cent, say "s" followed by the rest of the word.When C is followed by e, i, or y, say the soft /s/

3. Hard G:

When G is followed by a, o, or u, say the hard /g/ sound. For example, for goat, say "g" followed by the rest of the word.

4. Soft G:

When G is followed by e, i, or y, say the soft /j/ sound. For example, for giant, say "j" followed by the rest of the word.

BR blend. BR = /br/ (as in brand)

Words:bread, brush, brave, brown, bridge, bright, break, brother, bring, brick, brand, broom, brunch, bracelet, broadcast, brittle, breathe, brew, bristle, browse, broad, bristle, brisk, brook, broken, bramble, brunch, brain, brittle, bravery.

Read the sentences .Then underline the word "br".

☐ She baked fresh bread for breakfast.

☐ He used a brush to paint the canvas.

☐ The brave knight rescued the princess.

☐ The brown bear wandered through the forest.

☐ They crossed the bridge over the river.

☐ The bright sun shone down on the field.

☐ Be careful not to break the glass.

☐ My brother loves to play soccer.

☐ Can you bring me a glass of water?

☐ The wall was made of solid brick.

☐ She decided to brand her new product.

☐ He swept the floor with a broom.

Story -Once upon a time, in a small village, there lived a brave boy named **Brennan**. One day, he decided to explore the mysterious **br**idge that crossed the river behind his house. As he approached, he noticed a shiny **br**ass bell hanging from the archway.

Curiosity piqued, he gave it a gentle **br**ush with his fingers, and to his surprise, the bell rang beautifully. Suddenly, a **br**illiant light appeared, and a friendly dragon named **Bruno** emerged from the shadows. "Thank you for ringing my bell!" Bruno said, his scales shimmering in the sunlight. "I've been waiting for someone brave enough to explore this bridge."

Excitedly, Brennan climbed onto Bruno's back, and together they soared through the sky, discovering hidden valleys and sparkling lakes. They became the best of friends, promising to go on many adventures together, united by the magic of the bridge.

CR blend. CR = /cr/ (as in crash)
Words:

crab, cry, crown, cross, crash, crate, cream, crisp, crack, crawl, credit, crowd, crate, crate, crumble, crispy, crop, creep, crystal, crosswalk, crush, crayon, crown, crinkle, crutch, crate, crimson, croak, creak, cricket.

Say the blend "CR" .Then write the blend "CR".

Read the sentences .Then underline the word "CR".

☐ The crab scuttled across the sandy beach.

☐ She began to cry when she heard the news.

☐ The queen wore a beautiful crown.

☐ Please don't cross the street without looking.

☐ The car made a loud crash when it hit the wall.

☐ He carried the heavy crate to the truck.

☐ She added cream to her coffee.

☐ The apple was crisp and delicious.

☐ I heard a crack in the ice.

☐ The baby began to crawl on the floor.

☐ He needed credit for his hard work.

☐ A large crowd gathered for the concert.

Story-In a cozy little town, there lived a clever girl named **Cris**. One bright morning, she found a **cr**ystal pendant while playing in her backyard. It sparkled in the sunlight, and she felt a strange **cr**eative energy flowing through her.Curious about its magic,

Cris decided to wear the pendant and explore the nearby **cr**eek. As she walked along the water's edge, she noticed a **cr**ow perched on a branch, cawing loudly. "What do you want, little bird?" she asked.

To her amazement, the crow flew down and landed on her shoulder. "I can guide you to a secret **cr**anny in the woods," it said. Intrigued, Cris followed the crow through the trees until they arrived at a hidden clearing filled with **cr**imson flowers and **cr**ystalCris realized that the pendant had brought her here, and she promised to visit this magical place every day, cherishing her new feathered friend.

FR blend. FR = /fr/ (as in frog)

Words

frame, freight, fright, fringe, frill, fragile, from, frantic, frugal, frenzy, fruitcake, frigid, fragrance, frolic, fray, freckle, front, frypan, friction, fruitless, frostbite, funnel, fray, frank.,: frog, friend, fresh, fry, free, fruit, frost,

Say the blend "FR" .Then write the blend "FR".

Read the sentences .Then underline the word "FR".

☐ The frog jumped into the pond.

☐ She is my best friend.

☐ He enjoyed fresh fruits for breakfast.

☐ They decided to fry the potatoes for dinner.

☐ The birds fly free in the sky.

☐ She picked some fruit from the tree.

☐ The frost covered the grass in the morning.

☐ He painted the picture in a beautiful frame.

☐ The truck carried a heavy freight.

☐ The loud noise gave her a fright.

☐ She wore a lovely fringe on her jacket.

☐ The dress had a pretty frill at the bottom.

Story-In a bustling village, there lived a friendly frog named **Freddie**. Freddie loved to play in the **fr**agrant flowers that bloomed around the pond. One sunny afternoon, he decided to organize a **fr**og race for all his friends. He hopped around excitedly, calling out, "Come one, come all! Let's have some fun!"

The frogs gathered at the pond, their **fr**ogs sparkling in the sunlight. Freddie explained the rules: they would race from one side of the pond to the other. With a loud **fr**oar, the race began! Freddie leaped with all his might, feeling the cool breeze against his skin.

As they raced, they spotted a **fr**ightened little fish trapped in a net. Without hesitation, Freddie and his friends stopped to help. Together, they freed the fish, who thanked them profusely. "You may not have won the race," said the fish, "but you're all true champions!"Freddie smiled, realizing that friendship was the real victory.

DR blend. DR = /dr/ (as in drop)

Words:

drive,drop, drip, dress, dragon, drought, drift, drive, drape, drain, driftwood, dribble, drone, dredge, drizzle, drench, drag, drip, drab, drama, dread, drumming, drape, dressmaker, drumstick, dreary, dramatic, drench. draw, drum, dream

Say the blend "DR" .Then write the blend "DR".

Say the blend "DR" .Then write the blend "DR".

Read the sentences .Then underline the word "DR".

☐ She loves to draw pictures in her notebook.

☐ The drummer kept the beat perfectly.

☐ He had a strange dream last night.

☐ They decided to drive to the beach.

☐ Be careful not to drop the fragile vase.

☐ The faucet began to drip all night.

☐ She wore a beautiful dress to the party.

☐ The dragon flew over the mountain.

☐ The drought affected the entire region.

☐ The leaves began to drift down in autumn.

☐ He loves to drive fast cars.

☐ She will drape the fabric over the table.

Story-In a quaint little village, there lived a dreamer named **Drew**. Every night, he would look up at the stars and imagine adventures beyond the **dr**ifting clouds. One evening, as he sat by the **dr**ainage pond, he noticed something shining beneath the surface. Curious, he reached in and pulled out a beautiful,
silver **dr**agonfly.

"Thank you for rescuing me!" said the dragonfly. "I'm **Draco**, and I can grant you one wish for your kindness." Drew's eyes sparkled with excitement. "I wish to explore the world beyond this village! With a gentle flutter, Draco lifted Drew into the sky. They soared over **dr**amatic mountains and shimmering rivers, discovering places Drew had only dreamed of.

As they returned home, Drew realized that the best partof his adventure was the friendship he had formed. "I'll always cherish this day, Draco!" he said, knowing that dreams can become a reality with a little courage and a friend.

GR blend. GR = /gr/ (as in grab)

Words:

grand, group, ground, grow, grip, great, grain, grab, grim, graduate, gremlin, greenhouse, grind, groan, greet, groovy, gravel, grimace, grasp, grumpy, grapevine, graffiti, grayish, grimy, granted, griddle, grate

Read the sentences .Then underline the word "GR".

☐ The grass is soft under my feet.

☐ The sky turned a deep gray before the storm.

☐ She picked a sweet grape from the vine.

☐ He had a big grin on his face.

☐ The grand building was a sight to see.

☐ Our group is going on a trip together.

☐ The ground was covered in fallen leaves.

☐ Plants need sunlight to grow properly.

☐ He couldn't get a good grip on the slippery rope.

☐ The movie was really great!

☐ The farmer harvested the grain in autumn.

☐ Please grab a chair and sit down.

Story-In a green valley filled with tall **gr**ass and blooming flowers, there lived a brave girl named **Grace**. One day, while wandering near the **gr**avel path, she stumbled upon a **gr**and old oak tree. Its trunk was thick and **gr**oovy, and it looked like it had many stories to tell.

Curious, Grace placed her hand on the tree's rough bark. Suddenly, she heard a soft whisper. "Help me, dear child," it said. Grace looked around and noticed a little **gr**iffin tangled in some vines. "Oh no! I'll help you!" she exclaimed. With gentle hands, Grace carefully untangled the vines. The **gr**iffin flapped its wings in joy, and it said, "Thank you, brave girl! I will grant you a wish!" Grace thought for a moment and wished for more adventures.

With a flutter of its wings, the **gr**iffin lifted her into the sky, and together they soared through the valley, ready for new adventures.

PR blend. PR = /pr/ (as in print)
Words:

prompt, pretty, prize, program, press, project, principal, process, protect, presence, pretty, primate, prank, profound, prowl, propane, pristine, prepare, prevent, printout, printer, proceed, productivity, prance, preheat, preview,pray, print, proud, price, prince, .

Say the blend "PR". Then write the blend "PR".

Say the blend "PR". Then write the blend "PR".

Read the sentences .Then underline the word "PR".

☐ We gather to pray before meals.

☐ She used a printer to make copies of her work.

☐ He felt proud of his achievements.

☐ The price of the book was surprisingly low.

☐ The prince rode his horse through the village.

☐ The teacher gave a prompt response to the question.

☐ The garden was filled with pretty flowers.

☐ She won a prize for her art project.

☐ They will program the robot to follow commands.

☐ Please press the button to start the machine.

☐ They are working on a new project together.

Story-In a ibrant village, there lived a curious girl named **Priya**. One sunny morning, she decided to go on an adventure in the nearby **pr**airie. With a basket in hand, she set off to **pr**ick some wildflowers.

The **pr**airie's beauty amazed her, with colorful blooms dancing in the gentle breeze.

As she wandered deeper, Priya stumbled upon a **pr**oud peacock displaying its magnificent feathers. "Hello, beautiful bird!" she exclaimed.

The peacock strutted around and invited her to follow him to a hidden **pr**eek nearby

Excitedly, Priya followed, discovering a **pr**istine pond filled with sparkling water. As she bent down to drink, she noticed a shiny **pr**incess pendant shimmering at the bottom. "What a wonderful find!" she thought. The peacock nodded, "You've discovered the treasure of the prairie.

Keep it safe, and it will bring you good luck!"

Priya smiled, grateful for her adventure and the new friend she made.

WR blend. WR = /wr/ (as in wrap)

Words:

wry, wriggle, writer, wrinkled, wre,wrench, wring, wrap, wrangle, wreck, wristwatch,ath, wrestle, wrinkle, wretched, wrangler, wrinkly, wroth, wrangle, write-off, wrapper, wrapped, wrens, wrenching, write-up,write, wrong, wrap, wrist, wreath, wrinkle.

Say the blend "WR" .Then write the blend "WR".

Read the sentences .Then underline the word "Wr".

☐ Please write your name on the paper.

☐ It's wrong to cheat on a test.

☐ She will wrap the gift in colorful paper.

☐ He wore a bracelet on his wrist.

☐ The holiday wreath decorated the door.

☐ There was a wrinkle in his shirt.

☐ He used a wrench to fix the bike.

☐ She had to wring out the wet towel.

☐ They started to wrangle over the rules.

☐ The car was a complete wreck after the accident.

☐ He checked the time on his wristwatch.

Story- In abright and beautiful garden, a clever little rabbit named **Bruno** loved to explore. One sunny morning, he decided to visit his friend **Cris** the **cr**ow. As Bruno hopped through the **grass**, he heard a gentle **fr**olicking sound nearby.Curious, he followed the sound and found **Fiona**, a **fr**og, jumping near a small **dr**ain. "What are you doing?" asked Bruno. Fiona smiled and said, "I'm practicing my jumps!"

"Let's all play together!" Bruno suggested. Soon, they invited **Prudence**, the **pr**oud peacock, and **Greg**, the **gr**assy lizard, to join in. They played games, racing and leaping in the sunshine.

Phonics " S " Blends Guide

What is a Blend?

A blend is when two or more consonants come together to create a new sound.
For example, in the word "st" (as in "stop"), the letters "s" and "t" combine

to make one sound.

Common "S" Blends:

1. Sc- Blend:

The sound made when the letters s and c come together.

Example words: scoop, scan, scout.

2. Sk- Blend:

The sound made when the letters s and k come together.

Example words: skill, skate, sketch.

3. Sm- Blend:

The sound made when the letters s and m come together.

Example words: smile, smoke, small.

4. . Sn- Blend:

The sound made when the letters s and n come together.

Example words: snow, snake, snail.

5. Sp- Blend:

The sound made when the letters s and p come together.

Example words: spin, spoon, speed.

6.St- Blend:

The sound made when the letters s and t come together.

Example words: stop, star, straw.

7. Sw- Blend:

The sound made when the letters s and w come together.

Example words: swim, sweet, swim.

How to Pronounce Blends:

1. Start Slowly:

Begin by saying each consonant sound slowly. For example, for st, say

"s-s-t" and then blend them together until it sounds like "st."

2. Practice with Your Mouth:

Pay attention to how your mouth moves when saying each blend.
For the sl sound, your tongue should be near the top of your mouth,
just behind your teeth, to make the "l" sound while pronouncing the "s."

Tips for Mastering "S" Blends:

1. Use Visuals:

Associate each blend with a picture. For example, "st"
can be linked to a picture of a star or a stop sign.

2. Repeat Words:

Practice saying words with the same blend.
Make it a fun game to say words with the st blend
(e.g., "stop," "star," and "straw") and see how fast you can say them!

SC Blend . SC = /SC/ (as in scoop)
Words:

schedule, science, score, screen, scissors, scout,

sculpture, scrape, scratch, scold, scowl, scenery,

scoop, scout, scour, scandal, scar, scoop, scroll, script,

scratchy,sculptor, scurry, scissor, scent, scuttle,scare,

school, scale, scream,.

Say the blend "SC" .Then write the blend "SC".

Read the sentences .Then underline the word "SC".

☐ The loud noise might scare the children.

☐ I go to school every weekday.

☐ He stepped on the scale to check his weight.

☐ She let out a scream when she saw the spider.

☐ He wrapped the scarf around his neck.

☐ I need to check my schedule for tomorrow.

☐ Science class is always interesting.

☐ She got a high score on the test.

☐ The movie played on the big screen.

☐ The scout found a great camping spot.

☐ The sculpture in the park is beautiful.

Story-In a small town, there lived a clever boy named **Scott**. One day, while

exploring the **sc**enic hills near his home, he discovered a **sc**arred tree with

a peculiar **sc**ratch on its trunk. Curious, Scott leaned closer

and noticed something shiny hidden beneath the bark.

He gently scraped away the **sc**ab and uncovered a beautiful, ancient **sc**roll!

Excitedly, he opened it and found a map leading to a hidden treasure buried deep in

the **sc**arred forest.With his heart racing, Scott decided to follow the map.

He ventured throughthe **sc**ent of pine trees and over rocky paths,

 finally arriving at the spot markedWith a **sc**arlet "X."

After digging for a while, he unearthed a **sc**rumptious chest

filled with sparkling gems and golden coins.

Scott couldn't believe his luck! He hurried home to share

his adventure and the treasure with his family, grateful for the magical

 day in the **sc**enic hills.

SK Blend. SK= /SK/ (as in skip)
Words:

skateboarder, skincare, skateskateskate, sky, skirt, skill, scream,

skewer,sky, skirt, skill, scream, skewer, sketchbook, skyrocket, skincare,

skillful, skipole, skipping, sketchy, skitter, skirmish ,skim, skunk, skip,

skydiver, skillet, skeleton, skateboarding, skincare, sketch, ski, skew,

skit,

Say the blend "SK" . Then write the blend "SK".

Read the sentences .Then underline the word "SK".

☐ They love to skate at the park.

☐ The sky is blue and clear today.

☐ She wore a beautiful skirt to the party.

☐ He has a special skill in playing the guitar.

☐ I let out a scream when I saw the snake.

☐ She used a skewer to hold the vegetables.

☐ He likes to skim the surface of the water.

☐ The skunk sprayed when it felt threatened.

☐ They decided to skip the boring meeting.

☐ The skydiver jumped from the plane.

☐ She cooked eggs in a skillet.

☐ The skeleton in the science lab is interesting.

Story-In a quiet village, there lived a skilled young girl named Skye.

She had a passion for skating and spent every afternoon

gliding gracefully

on the smooth ice of the frozen lake. One winter day,

while practicing

*her spins, she not*iced something shiny at the edge of the skating rink.

Curious, Skye skated over and found a small, silver skate charm.

Excited, she picked it up and wished for the ability to perform

the most spectacular

skate moves. As soon as she made her wish, a gentle wind blew

through the trees,

and suddenly, she felt lighter and more agile.

With newfound confidence, Skye began to spin

and jump with ease.

The other villagers gathered to watch her mesmerizing performance.

They cheered and clapped as she executed breathtaking tricks.

Skye realized that her love for skating had brought her closer to her

community and filled her heart with joy.

SM Blend. SM = /SM/ (as in smart) Words:

smell, smash, smirk, smartly, smudge, smuggle, smock, smear, smirk, smoother, smeared, smattering, smelly, smog, smuggle, smallish, smattering, smock, smattering, smashed , soldering , smock, smartphone, smeary, smattering,smile, small, smoke, smart, smooth, .

Say the blend " SM" .Then write the blend " SM".

Read the sentences .Then underline the word "SM".

☐ She had a bright smile on her face.

☐ The puppy is small and cute.

☐ We could see smoke rising from the chimney.

☐ He is very smart for his age.

☐ The ice cream was smooth and creamy.

☐ The cookies had a lovely smell.

☐ He tried to smash the bug with his shoe.

☐ She wore a smirk after winning the game.

☐ He dressed smartly for the interview.

☐ There was a smudge on the window.

☐ They tried to smuggle the goods across the border.

Learn English Reading In Just 90 Days

Story: In a charming little town, there lived a small boy named Sam. Sam loved to spend his afternoons in the sunny small park near his home. One day, while playing with his friends, he discovered a smoky trail leading into the woods. Curious, Sam and his friends decided to follow it. As they walked deeper into the forest, they stumbled upon a smiling squirrel sitting on a branch. "Hello there!" squeaked the squirrel. "I'm Sophie, and I've lost my favourite acorn!" Sam wanted to help. "We can find it together!" he exclaimed. The group searched high and low, looking behind small bushes and beneath smelly leaves. Finally, they spotted the acorn under a smooth rock. Sophie was overjoyed and thanked Sam and his friends for their help. In return, she invited them to her tree for a small picnic. They spent the rest of the day enjoying snacks and laughter, grateful for their new furry friend.

SN Blend. SN = /SN/ (as in snow)

Words:

sniff, snuff, snatch, snicker, snide, snowy, sneaky, snub, snickered, sneer, snuggle, snappy, snapdragon, snazzy, snooze, snipes snoopy, snout,snack, snake, snow, snap, snore, snuggle, snip, snare, sneeze, snazzy, snarl, snail,

Say the blend "SN" .Then write the blend "SN".

Read the sentences .Then underline the word "SN".

☐ I love to have a snack after school.

☐ The snake slithered across the path.

☐ The snow covered the ground in winter.

☐ He heard a loud snap when he stepped on the twig.

☐ She started to snore during the movie.

☐ The puppy loves to snuggle on the couch.

☐ Please snip the paper along the lines.

☐ He set a snare to catch the rabbit.

☐ I had to sneeze during the meeting.

☐ She wore a snazzy outfit to the party.

☐ The dog began to snarl at the stranger.

☐ A snail moved slowly across the garden.

☐ He likes to sniff the flowers in spring.

SP Blend. SP = /SP/ (as in spoon)

Words:

spring, spill, spin, spider, splash, split, speech, special, spice, spark, sponge, sponsor,sparkle,spectacle, spicy, spectrum, spell, spine, sparkle, spicy, sprawl, sprout, spade, spirit, spout, speed ,space, spoon, sparkle, spot, sport,

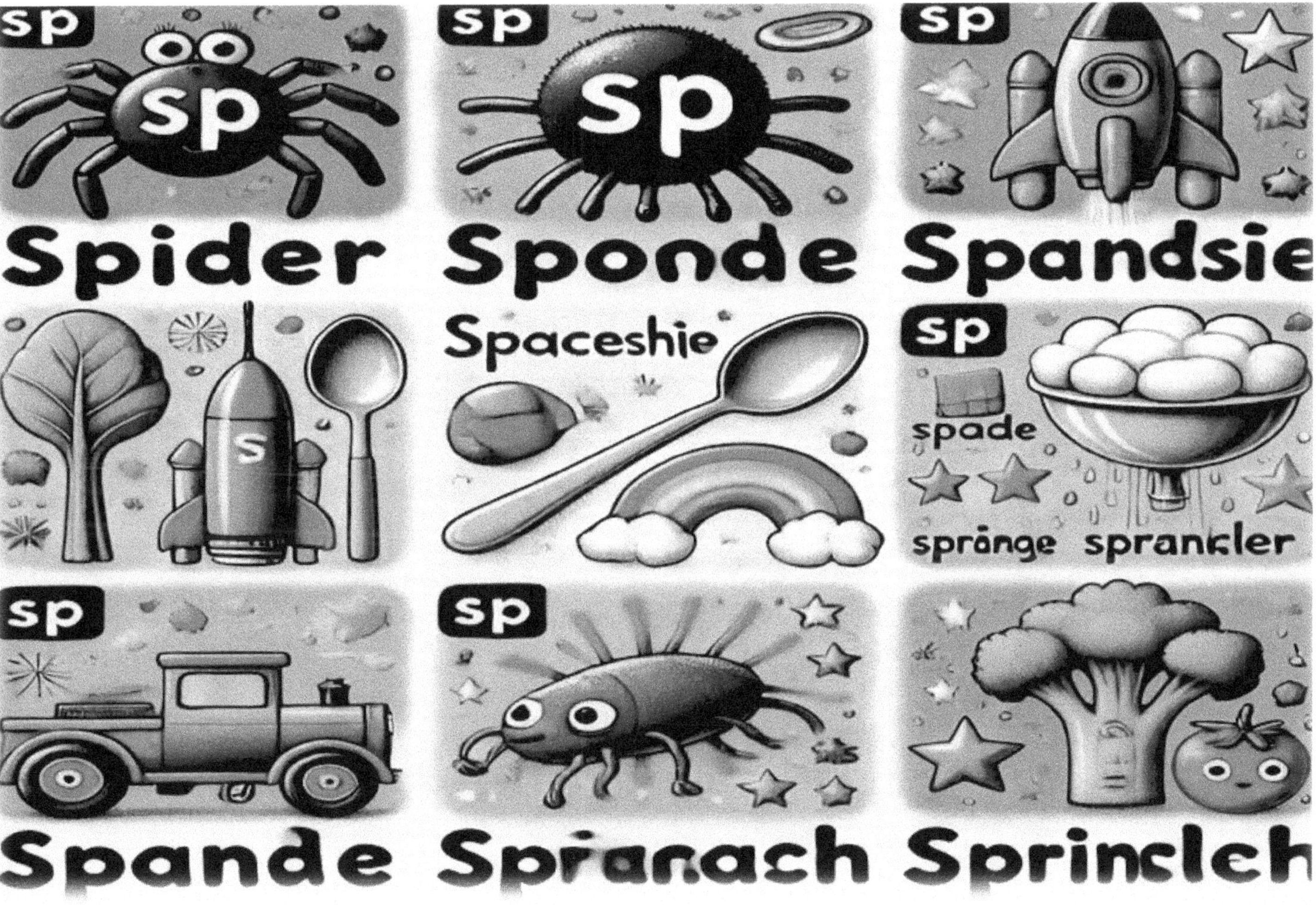

Say the blend "SP" .Then write the blend "SP".

Read the sentences .Then underline the word "SP".

- [ ] She stirred her soup with a spoon.
- [ ] The stars began to sparkle in the night sky.
- [ ] I found a bright spot on the wall.
- [ ] He enjoys playing sport on the weekends.
- [ ] The flowers bloom beautifully in spring.
- [ ] Be careful not to spill the milk.
- [ ] The wheel began to spin quickly.
- [ ] The spider spun a web in the corner.
- [ ] They made a big splash in the pool.
- [ ] Please split the cake into equal pieces.

Story-In a small town, there lived a boy named Spencer who loved .spend time in the park. One sunny afternoon, while playing with his friends, he discovered a spinning top hidden beneath a sprawling oak tree. Excitedly, he picked it up and noticed it had vibrant colours. "Let's have a spinning contest!" Spencer exclaimed. His friends gathered around as he placed the top on the ground and gave it a good spin. The to*p whirled and spun, creating a beautiful display of colours.*

As the top slowed down, a spirit appeared, sparkling with light. "Thank you for finding my top!" the spirit said. "In return for your kindness, I will grant you one wish!"

ST Blend . ST = /ST/ (as in star)
Words:

steam, strength, student, style, station,still,stone, stunning, stroll,

straight, studious street, stamp, story, step, starlight, steak, statue,star,

stop, stick, stand, storm, stash, stain, stumble, stork, stove, storage, staff,

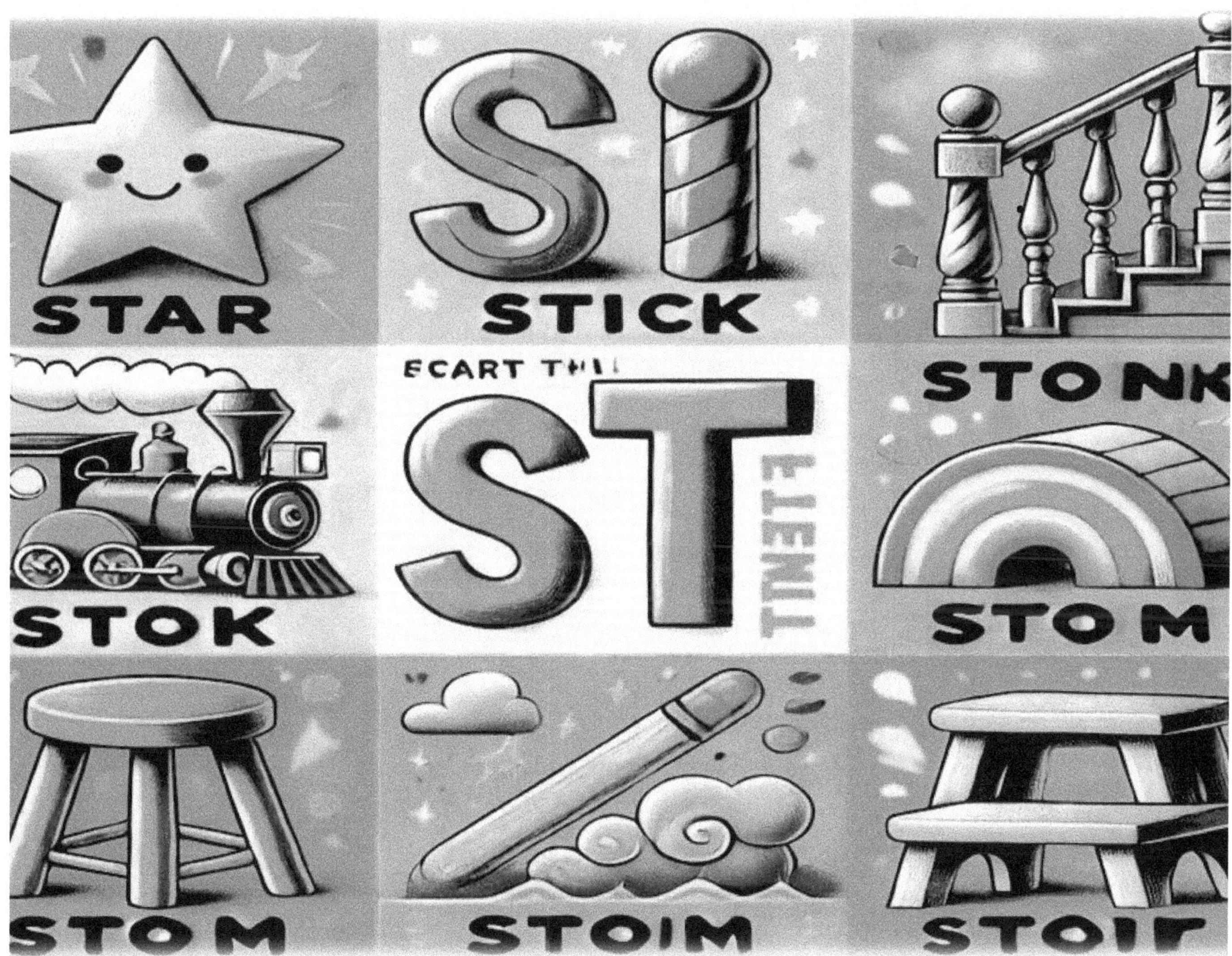

Say the blend "ST" .Then write the blend "ST".

Read the sentences .Then underline the word "ST".

☐ The star twinkled brightly in the night sky.

☐ Please stop talking during the movie.

☐ She used a stick to draw in the sand.

☐ You need to stand up straight.

☐ A storm is approaching the area.

☐ The lake was still and calm this morning.

☐ We walked down the busy street.

☐ He placed a stamp on the envelope.

☐ I love reading a good story before bed.

☐ Be careful with every step you take.

☐ The starlight made the night magical.

☐ We grilled a delicious steak for dinner.

Story-In a bustling town, there lived a little girl named Stella. She was known for her bright smile and adventurous spirit. One day, she discovered an old map tucked inside her grandmother's steamer trunk. It was marked with a big red "X" near the star-lit mountains. Excited, Stella gathered her friends, and they set off on a quest to find the hidden treasure. They travelled through streets lined with blooming flowers and

crossed a stream filled with sparkling water. As they reached the mountains, they encountered a storm,

but Stella encouraged everyone to stay brave. "We can do this together!" she said. Finally, they reached the spot marked on the map and started digging. To their surprise, they uncovered a stunning chest filled with colourful gems and gold coins! Stella and her friends cheered with delight, knowing this adventure would be a story they would share for years to com

SW Blend. SW = /SW/ (as in swim)
Words:

swarm, switch, swift, swirl, swish, swing, sweeten, swoop, swaddle,

swish, swindle, swelter, sway, swab, swish, swindle, swan, swaddle,

swishes, swoosh, swish, swig, swoon, swindle.,swim, sweet, swing,

sweater, swan,swipe

Say the blend "SW" . Then write the blend "SW".

Read the sentences .Then underline the word "SW".

- ☐ I love to swim in the ocean during summer.

- ☐ The cake was very sweet and delicious.

- ☐ The children enjoy playing on the swing.

- ☐ She wore a warm sweater to the picnic.

- ☐ A beautiful swan glided across the lake.

- ☐ Please swipe your card to enter.

- ☐ The bees began to swarm around the flowers.

- ☐ He decided to switch lanes while driving.

- ☐ The bird flew with a swift motion.

- ☐ The colours began to swirl together in the painting.

- ☐ She heard the swish of the basketball net.

Story-In a quiet village, there lived a young boy named Swami who loved to explore the nearby forest. One bright morning, he decided to go on a swimming adventure at the sparkling swamp just beyond the trees. As he approached the swamp, he noticed a family of swans gliding gracefully across the water. Swami waved at them and exclaimed, "Hello, beautiful swans!" he swans swam closer, curiously watching him. Suddenly, he spotted a swirling whirlpool in the distance. Intrigued, he waded into the shallow water, feeling the coolness on his feet. As he got closer, he noticed a shiny object at the bottom. It was a swimming medal! Excitedly, he dove down and retrieved it. "This must belong to someone who loves the swamp as much as I do!" he thought. Swami decided to find the owner and return the medal, cherishing his day of adventure.

Phonics " L " Blends Guide

What is a Blend? A blend is when two or more consonants come together to

create a new sound.

For example, in the word "cl" (as in "clay"),

the letters "c" and "l" combine to make one sound.

Common "L" Blends:

1. Bl- Blend: The sound made when the letters b and l come together.

Example words: blue, block, blush.

2.Pl- Blend:

The sound made when the letters p and l come together.
Example words: play, plate, plum.

3.Fl- Blend:

The sound made when the letters f and l come together.

Example words: flag, fly, flame.

4.Gl- Blend:

The sound made when the letters g and l come together.

Example words: glove, glue, glitter.

5.Cl- Blend:

The sound made when the letters c and l come together.

Example words: clay, cloud, clow

How to Pronounce Blends:

1. Start Slowly: **Begin by saying each consonant sound slowly. For example, for cl, say "c-l"and then blend them together until it sounds like "cl."**

2. Practice with Your Mouth:

Pay attention to how your mouth moves when saying each blend. For the fl sound, your upper teeth should gently touch your bottom lip to make the "f" sound before quickly adding the "l."

Tips for Mastering "L" Blends:

1. Use Visuals:

Associate each blend with a picture. For example, "cl" can be linked to a picture of a clown or a cloud.

2. Repeat Words:

Practice saying words with the same blend. Make it a fun game to say words with the cl blend (e.g., "clay," "cloud," and "clown") and see how fast you can say them!

Bl blend. Bl = /bl/ (as in black)

Words:

blaze, blend, bless, blood, blanket, blip, blare, blizzard, blade, bloom, blossom, bluff, blunt, blaze, blister,black, blue, blind, bless, block, bland, blink, bluster, blimp, blink, blot, bleep, bling, blubber, blip

Say the blend "BL" .Then write the blend "BL

Say the blend "BL" .Then write the blend "BL

Read the sentences .Then underline the word "BL".

☐ The black cat sat on the blue rug.

☐ She decided to bless her friends with gifts.

☐ The blind man walked confidently with his cane.

☐ They planned to block the path with chairs.

☐ The bland soup needed more seasoning.

☐ He blinked in surprise at the sudden noise.

☐ The blaze in the fireplace warmed the room.

☐ They will blend different colors for the project.

☐ The blanket kept her warm during the night.

☐ A blip on the radar indicated something unusual.

☐ The loud blare of the horn startled everyone.

Story: In a bright forest, a little bluebird named Blossom loved to sing.

One day, while flying near a black rock,

she heard a soft bleating sound.

Curious, she followed the sound and found

 a black lamb stuck in some bushes."Oh dear!

Let me help you!" said Blossom.

She used her sharp beak to carefully pull away the bushes.

With a grateful bleat, the lamb wiggled free.

"Thank you, Blossom! I'm Blake.

Let's be friends!"From that day on,

 Blossom and Blake explored the forest,

singing and playing together beneath the blue sky,

creating a bond that would last forever.

Excitedly, Brennan climbed onto Bruno's back,

 and together they soared through the sky,

 discovering hidden valleys and sparkling lakes.

They became the best of friends, promising to go on many

 adventures together, united by the magic of the bridge.

Excitedly, Brennan climbed onto Bruno's back,

 and together they soared through the sky,

 discovering hidden valleys and sparkling lakes.

 They became the best of friends,

 promising to go on many adventures together,

united by the magic of the bridge.

PL blend. PL = /pr/ (as in plum)

Words:

plummet, plug, plateau, plaster,pluck, plu, plea,plus, plunge, plunge, plait, plank, plead, pleat, plow, plod, plink, plush, pleat, pled plaza, plankton, plastic, plummet, play, plant, plum, plane, plate, plural

Say the blend "PL" .Then write the blend "PL".

Read the sentences .Then underline the word "Pl".

The children love to play in the park.

☐

She decided to plant flowers in the garden.

☐

The plum was ripe and juicy.

☐

He boarded the plane to New York.

☐

She set the table with a beautiful plate.

☐

He tried to pluck the ripe fruit from the tree.

☐

The plump cat lounged in the sun.

☐

They need to plow the fields before planting.

☐

He made a heartfelt plea for help.

☐

They decided to add dessert plus coffee.

☐

She took a plunge into the deep end of the pool.

Story- Story: In a small village, a playful puppy named
loved to play in the plenty of plants around. One sunny day,
he spotted a plan that looked different from the others. Curious, he
sniffed it and accidentally knocked over a plant pot.

"Oh no!" exclaimed his friend Lila,
a little girl who loved to plant flowers.
They quickly gathered the dirt and planted the flowers again.
"Let's make this place beautiful!" said Pluto. Together,
they planted colorful flowers and laughed,
creating a lovely garden that everyone in the village admired.

Phonics

FL blend. FL = /fl/ (as in flag)

Words:

flinch, flirt, flake, flip, float, flounder, flock, flush, flash, flare, flap, flame, flare, flume, flourish, flute, flurry, fleck, flee, flimsy, flint, flounder, flint ,flag, flat, fly, flip, flood, flower, flake, flee,

Say the blend "FL" .Then write the blend "FL".

Read the sentences .Then underline the word "FL".

☐ The flag waved in the gentle breeze.

☐ The pancake was perfectly flat on the plate.

☐ Birds fly south for the winter.

☐ He tried to flip the pancake without making a mess.

☐ The heavy rain caused a flood in the streets.

☐ She loved the scent of fresh flowers in spring.

☐ A snowflake fell gently to the ground.

☐ The rabbit decided to flee from the fox.

☐ He would flinch at sudden loud noises.

☐ They began to flirt during the school dance.

☐ The flakes of snow covered the ground.

Story-One day, a little fairy named **Flora**

flew into a **fl**ower-filled garden.

The flowers danced in the gentle **fl**ow of the breeze, and

Flora loved the sight. She had a magical **fl**ute that could make

the flowers bloom even brighter.As she played a sweet melody,

the flowers **fl**ourished and turned **fl**amboyant colors.

Suddenly, she noticed a sad flower drooping in the corner.

"Don't worry! I'll help you!" said Flora. She

played a cheerful tune, and the flower perked

up, smiling brightly. Together,

they filled the garden with joy and laughter.

GL blend. GL = /Gl/ (as in glass)

Words-

glob, gleeful, glade, gloat, glare, gland, glock, glimmer, glowworm, glutton, global,glass, globe, glow, glide, glue, glint, glance,glib,glitter, glee, gleam, glitch, glimmer, glide, , glossary, gleefully, glucose, glossary, glacial.

Say the blend "GL" .Then write the blend "GL".

Read the sentences .Then underline the word "GL".

☐ The glass shattered on the floor.

☐ She loves to collect different globes.

☐ The stars began to glow brightly at night.

☐ The bird will glide smoothly through the air.

☐ He used glue to fix the broken toy.

☐ The sun made a glint on the water.

☐ The decorations glittered in the sunlight.

☐ They squealed with glee when they won.

☐ A gentle gleam of light caught her eye.

☐ The video game had a glitch that needed fixing.

☐ The diamonds will glimmer in the light.

Story:

In a cozy little cottage, a girl named Gloria loved to collect glittering stones by the river.

One day, while searching for shiny treasures, she found a glass jar half-buried in the sand.

Curious, she picked it up and noticed it was glowing softly.

"What a magical jar!" she exclaimed. As she opened it, colorful globes floated into the air, sparkling like stars.
"Wow! I can make wishes!" Gloria said excitedly.
She closed her eyes, made a wish, and watched

as the globes danced around her, making her garden the most beautiful place in the village.

CL blend. CL = /cl/ (as in clap)
Words-

clothe, clumsy, clench, cloven, clench, clinker, clerk, clamor, clifftop, climber,clamp, clap, class, clean, climb, clip, clock, cloud, clover, clue, close, clumsy, clutch, clipper, clink, cling, clatter, clear, clout, clamor, clasp,

Say the blend "CL" .Then write the blend "CL".

Read the sentences .Then underline the word "CL".

☐ The clamp held the wood securely in place.

☐ The audience began to clap after the performance.

☐ The teacher assigned homework to the class.

☐ She wanted to clean her room before guests arrived.

☐ He decided to climb the tall tree in the park.

☐ She used a clip to hold her papers together.

☐ The clock on the wall chimed at noon.

☐ A fluffy cloud drifted across the sky.

☐ The clover patch was full of four-leafed luck.

☐ He found a clue that led to the treasure.

☐ Please close the door quietly.

Sight Words

Set 1	Set 2	Set 3	Set 4
Is	Put	These	All
You	But	Again	Our
Look	Now	There	the
At	Want	Could	To
Are	Him	Because	Go
Play	Will	Their	You
The	By	Away	He
I	Has	Your Do	He
A	Am	Walk	Have
Like	Other	His	Here
My	Called	Has	Come
All	Into	Be	They
Some	About	Words	Old
Can	Out	Some	Any
See	Write	Two	Only
We	From	Would	What
Big	May	Write	Or
With	Every	First	Up
Where	Live	Another	Us
In	Them	Does	Soon
Little	People	Colour	Our
These	Then		Milk